HAPPY HOUR AT THE MISERY BAR

SEAN L. MACRO

DAGDA PUBLISHING

Dagda Publishing Ltd
85 St Stephens Road
Nottingham, UK
NG2 4JR

www.dagdapublishing.co .uk
www.facebook.com/dagdapublishing
www.twitter.com/dagdapublishing
www.dagdapublishing.tumblr.com
All enquiries: info@dagdapublishing.co.uk

For Katie

Contents

One, Matchstick Pessimist

I am squalor.

I dwell on the spark of a match that –
Soils the clean shirt of the night.
I am your mocking alarm clock.
I am a city pigeon stained by countryside.
I am "this train is being held here to regulate the service"
I am puff pastry, I am diet coke.
I am "Unfortunately your application has been unsuccessful this time"
I am your lost bankcards.
I am awkward glances
I am the beautiful blossom boy at Stepney Green
I am a broken battered toy, a Slut on the Game
I am an exchanged stare
I am heartache
I am longing
I am your favourite child
I am your worst enemy.

I behold the sun as a hungover old man
And force him to surrender his pale daughter
And in doing so I shall sully the corridors of Angel throats
Just as white waves choke sad sea
Allowing only a tuneless whisper to crawl, note by note
From 'neath a muted memory.

Leaving what in this wretched merry place?
Only my reprimand.
But should I find that I descend in stature from -
A great wood to a splinter
Then I shall laugh, laying
In wait, sealed away
Ready to strike,

And paint the dark.

Parched

Today -
Moments seem to slip through fingers
Like so much dirty water,
Talking to illness -
At the bottom of a well.
Like so much dirty water
Wearing new clothes -
Trying on new streams
Joining new banks -
As ever, feeling old hat.

Today -
Rhyme has been ruined
Like so much rust
Aching on brave red lips.
Decayed, praying
For some naked dream
To resuscitate -
The elderly flicker behind
Its defeated eyes.

Today -
She stumbles feebly
Across a thought, drifting
Not quite able, though trying -
To open the key with a lock.
But it's harder than dirty water, harder than -
Finding yesterday on the clock.

Clock-Leisure

I watched minds age -
Idyll, to idle.
Faces
Like yawning memories.
Weary eyes,
With -
Furrowed brows,
Furnished by time

Trying to embrace the ghost
Of infancy, instead
Grasping for the glass
That cynicism poured for -

Milky innocence.

With -

Cheap whiskey,
That -
Tastes a touch too cheap.

I'm Fine

You cracked the eggshell of my mind,
And now I find
The torture was just a pose.
Didn't you know?
You're just a statue wearing clothes

This is the silver season of the lonely spark
Where madness comes out to play,
In black sun treason so dark -
That I fade, awaiting another day.

I tried to plant the seed
But the night strangled me
In pale death-light,
I was alone.

In solar symmetry
Sorrow bites me sharp,
And draws dark blood
To please a silent harp

The dust of a lunar scar
Powder white, and cold -
Tears open the sky
Of a world that's not mine

And in that chasm
I'm aching,
Under the weight
Of your nothingness.

On Receiving a Ransom Note for a Crumbled Queen

Oh it must be rumbled the rosy rouse!
Of this devil's pale sky mask,
Smiling, yet stood accused,
Of selling the hopeful hip flask's
Sober secret.

Fuck you.

Your plastic poise promises -
That which it can't deliver
A silver sea that withers,
swimming in silver quivers.
A solvent that can't seal seams, seeming
To aspire to be heard not seen -
In a plastic crown, this crumbled queen,
Is blinded by the painless peel of your paint,
Of your bought beauty beyond taint!
Pretence is your husband's name,
A marriage of shame,
his pearls detained.
He dances like a jester in your bland monarchy,
And kisses the pearls that choke mediocrity,
Of all the powdered poofs he is the most pretty!
A blade of green in your grey-scale city.

Oh but still you request he returns,
To put on ice this passion that burns
And put his silly dreams to bed
Blushing quirks, more thought than said.
Against the grain this slight return -
Alights here, for a station in the dark.
Your voice raises cause for concern,
Dripping false from a question mark.
Have a quiet word with silent applause,
You'll hear no concern left for your cause.

Rotten Fruit

I've stitched my fame with malaise
Not sure if it healed the delusion -
I still wake up anonymous.
I've spent my days
Tottering round dying -
Starved of glamour
Begging to react
Against something.

I visited my smile
Took a holiday there,
A place I barely know
Where parents are pleased
And trains run on time.

But the ship sinks my iceberg.
I'm still scared of the dark,
I don't like to walk home
What's wrong with a man
After company?
I'm just sick of the sound of my own silence.

I float round the afternoons in a cloud
Padded, blowing raspberries at the insecurity
Of knowing nothing can protect me -
Only delay, delay the rupture of the wound

A mental scab,
Dressed in the trauma of the telephone ringing.

What's wrong with a man all alone?
Everything else is too fucking loud.

I don't fit the bill she said
And I wouldn't have minded, but they
Switched off my water.
I had a prescription once.
That helped for a little while

(is that too close to the bone?)
But you were already aware of that

Not
That I was the one to tell you
So cut the shit.

It was never a threat
Just as long as you're aware -
I promised I'd fall in love with you.
And I am, completely
But won't you please stop trying to call me
Please, not today
Its distracting me. I'm trying to remember
Where I put the safety net you came with.

Sleep's For the Poor

Why must you wake me at 9 A.M?
There is nothing for me in this hollow hour.
Fear treads on the soles of shadows rushing
Transparent, here the percussive clockwork of routine -
Oils heart motors and buttons collars.

Fear lines their wallets, the same
Fear wet roasting birthday cards
That spit back sticky pork bile
In a mutually assured disgust.

Why must you wake me at midnight?
Above, the moon flushes scarlet in sympathy
As my attention is drawn to
A graveyard of my sweethearts, their voices
An indignant static hiss
Mocking me for everything I have learned, and praising
The things I have pretended to know.

From the teenage window
Of the room they rent in my skull
They see me as I am at this moment -
A ticking corpse in a warm crypt

And find dull hilarity in the fact
That I have to be up in the morning.

The Sentiment of Sediment

Where is my welcome respite from the bitter breeze
Of bad news coming like the post of another person?

You are so very questionable,
And yet you only ask answers.

I still can't bear to remember your face.

Wrought from fair china, that immaculate smile
Carved on a cruel whim -
Is thinner than the heartbeat
Asleep in the cauldron of winter.

You found a way for me to undress under the moon
And melt away my anxiety and fragile demeanour,
For a time you even helped me to accept
The false membership of a declining generation.

And though I'd still like to rewind and adopt a new face
found in the footage of a memory
Taped over some old cinema film,
With sentiment dripping from the source

I simply can't let myself go
And forget them -
those that I loved
With lies as perfect as Broadway shows.

Now my reality is the realm of the moonlight habit
But you know I love you still,
And would do anything
Just to see your pot-the-black grin.

That pebble beach holiday -
I still have the scar on my knee!
From when we both fell over together
And even I flashed a rare smile.

Still Pure

I taste your green tea breath when I kiss you
Mine I imagine, spearmint and continental lager.
The monotony of grey coach seats staring
Back at me recedes,

When your pale pink face melts into view.
My eyes catch you by the station, a wandering photograph.
I am exhausted, filth is caked -
Into my eyes and polka-dot shirt

But your gentle embrace
Reminds me even a king
Is happily naked,
Beneath his clothes.

You're a tin foil fragile lover.
You ramble beautifully,
Composing symphonies
That play to the beat of your breath

We run rampant
On a shoe-string budget.
Happily joined together in a bow (although)
I still can't tie my laces.

Sometimes I watch you sleep easily
Hoping your mind might leak -
A cloudy cotton dream, in which
I don't speak quite so clumsily

So that I could explain just how much you mean to me.

Midday on a Christmas Evening

Thin crown of a gentle pier
Skeletal.
I find myself kissed by a polluted star
Far away from the fairer few
Numb the scent of her sound;
Silver.

Alphabet

A burning beacon caught catastrophic
Defeated, embers.
Fame grapples humility in jewellery
Kaleidoscopic lids line
Mr Nameless' oracle portals
Queen Red spies trivial tenements
Undying, vacant.
We xenogenesis, youthless zenith.

The Big Issue

Lately it's getting harder and harder
To work out what I need to say to you

As I wander past calloused trees
Roasted by summer heat just to become
Ready meals in winter's freezer,
I chance upon it – the reluctant phrase.

The rheumatic tune of a busker's harmonica
Wrenches me from the thought before its mine.
I don't mind, the dopey hum of it draws a smile
So I put a fifty pence piece in his hat's empty belly,

Hoping I've bought enough piece of mind for both of us.
Hours later, I'm sat alone at six A.M. in Victoria Park
The sun is wrestling with lime-scale clouds
And it's starting to get really cold.
I open a can of beer, bought from Sainsbury's
The night before. Then I remember -

I don't even know where you live now anyway.

Piccadilly Squares at the Hoxton Circus

Maybe just a shadow in the
Shape of London calls me back.
The well-worn alleyways
I have danced and crawled home on
Now feel like the burst capillaries that go unwashed
By the version of the Thames pouring
Into the powder smeared basin
Of a certain someone growing old disgracefully.

The Topshop princesses that
March to the beat of a receipt
Written in 4/4
(I wonder what they do that for?)
Wear kind daisy smiles
That turn to flower-on-fire scowls
When I politely point out -
I know where they bought their names from.

And the men are even worse,
Phosphorus pretenders with as much
Sparkle as flat cola.
They talk shit without value; it festers
Leaking from their mouths
Like processed cheese oozing from a burger.
And just how do they imagine the working people
Their dedication to cool evicts,

Bare strung wailers in the humility of night?
Or the actuality of bankrupt teeth
Chattering sharp on heartless late shifts.

As I climb the jacket of a skyscraper -
Numbed by the thin embrace of
A polystyrene coffee morning,
I laugh at just how tired the life they desire is.

A Hindsight Dream

Clarity called; I could not hear her...
I was far from fair moments
Where rust doesn't fall,
From a sky without song.

I heard only wails, wailing
SHRIEKS
exploding
Like flimsy lightning.

Unravelled now, all but picked away
The blood of a psyche
Half-healed this purple shame,
Withering into obscurity.

But see how it leaks into wounded view -
Twice as visible and vulnerable
As it would be
If left to fester undisturbed,

In the evil cell
Of my noon-night memory
Just like grape skin fermenting -
In the pit of a cheap wine.

A strange rain weeps now, kissing my brow.
Steam hisses and howls at the touch
Of my extinguished thought trail,
And I find myself again twenty-one.

But beneath the frail mask
Of my jester's grin,
I am still a quivering malleable soul.
Sealing myself off, brick by brick

In the blue-eyed loneliness of youthful design.

Brother

There's always a tyrant in a baggy blazer looking
To collect my teeth over some sharp remark.
And now I see my own lecherous flaws feeding on you
My little brother. I see your fresh blushing agony,
Bright and scarred as our pockmarked sun.

Because our London has hand sanitiser in its eye.
But I'll do the best I can to soothe you, by learning
To cash cheques with the edge of my recycled heart.
I'll even try to imitate happiness through the veneer of this keyboard,
So that my serotonin might gleam in the smile of your refreshed page.

That isn't real. This is real.
Trust me, I'm older than you
So I know for a fact that
I don't know what I'm talking about.

Company Procedure

Uniform.
Make your bargain
Then cuddle up to
Those stale hours.

Even I,
A strait-jacket phony
Smiling my penny smile
Kiss its mouth.

Its dull chain strangles
The gasping hide
Of my shoe,

As if that could prove
That I'm not just another animal.
My once wild ambition
Wears a blue collar,
Tied to a greasy dream.

There it shivers
Bald and sick,
Snapping pencil vertebrae
In brittle lament.

Opaque

Your jewels they shine like cardboard
As they size up the gentle beacon of surrender
That I offer as an umbrella,
Amidst the thankless cloud of evening.

The shadowed begging turnstile
Admitted you into the dark, where
In eloquence you met me -
Wearing my tuxedo thank you.

You washed away my opinions with detergent,
A masterstroke of vanity that -
Your children blush over
Because they don't understand

Why their daddy is gone,
And why my ring wears your hand.

Ghosts of the Playground

I've decided I'm leaving on a boat.
Please excuse me if this has reached you
After my departure.
You see, I've borrowed a boat &
Recruited a crew of fair weather angels

Dust is caked into their ancient teeth
& the bruised offerings
That they hold out -
Only to have their arms bitten off
Are floating beneath us

Free for anybody to take
As theirs.

Just as all should be.

Except a migraine painting dresses me
As the lonely leader of a drunk gang that -
Taunts me as I was, a freckled foetus.
Recoiling
I try to throw my dream to the cackling foam
Only to find I have never had one to give.

What happened to the Stones?

Is this the best we can do?
I mean I know the sun didn't always shine
In the sixties. But now
The pest of currency buzzes like flies
Vomiting on the warm carcass of *Gimme Shelter*.

Give me shelter.
From your bloated reign as
Transvestite dinosaur kings showing off
Freshly dyed hair on the hit parade.

The world leans in with the wind to listen
To that electric guitar ringing
Those same old muscular tunes,
Waiting for a feral crescendo

That never arrives.

Would You Like a Drink?

Your eyes lingered long enough -
To catch a glimpse
Of silver, glinting like
Pregnant madness
In the pulse of my soul.

And it spoke with time
To a beat for hours
Saying:

"We are but a benign tapestry,
Our loneliness is only a mask
For the false consciousness
Oh no wait, I meant confidence
Found at the bottom of a hip flask."

Senile

My mind, untroubled by the haunting of sleep -
Wanders further into scentless water
Where red thought exhumes a cultured sip
From the fossil memory of a skinny dip.

My brow is twisted in confused delight,
Uncertain of the sad faced flight
Of my three day elder friend whom
Is not broken, but will not mend.

The plucking of a fragile tune
Bends with me on time's avenues
Lost, looking for the street -
That both of us can gladly choose.

The searing pain of a lukewarm bath
Calls me out, and kisses my mask
One of several, the muscular pretender -
That sobs away watching Eastenders.

There's a knock. An eye is
Leering through my open mouthed letter box.
I creep onto the landing, only to hear
The metallic thud of its lips reuniting.

There's nothing there but today's newspaper,
Strange, I haven't paid for those in weeks.

About The Author

Sean L. Macro is a writer of poetry and short fiction. He has been published in both Dagda Publishig's online poetry blog, and Dead Beats Literary Blog, amongst other venues. This is his debut collection.

**

For more publications by Dagda Publishing Ltd, please visit
www.dagdapublishing.co.uk/shop